KT-496-958

Contents

Words that appear in the glossary are printed in **boldface** type the first time they occur in the text.

The streets of Tokyo are busy with activity.

WELCOME TO ☼ MY COUNTRY
JAPAN

Written by: Harlinah Whyte and Nicole Frank
Editors: Cheryl Sim and Melvin Neo
Designer: Benson Tan
Photo research: Thomas Khoo

PHOTO CREDITS
Alamy/Bes Stock: 3 (centre), 5, 7, 11, 15, 17 (bottom), 19, 22,
    25, 27, 29, 38
Bes Stock: 3 (top), 4, 6, 10, 20, 30, 31
Corbis: 9
Getty Images: 12, 33, 39, 41
Haga Library: 26, 32 (both)
Hutchison Library: 2, 8 (all), 17 (top), 18, 28, 35, 36
Photobank Photolibrary: 43
Photolibrary: cover, 1, 3 (bottom), 14, 23, 24, 37, 40, 45
Topham Picturepoint: 13, 16, 21, 34

This edition published in 2010
by Franklin Watts

Designed and originated by
Marshall Cavendish International (Asia) Pte Ltd
Copyright © Marshall Cavendish International (Asia) Pte Ltd 2010
Marshall Cavendish is a trademark of Times Publishing Limited.

Franklin Watts
338 Euston Road
London NW1 3BH

Dewey number 952'.05

ISBN 978 1 4451 0199 6

Franklin Watts is a division of Hachette Children's Books,
an Hachette UK company.
www.hachette.co.uk

Printed in Malaysia

Welcome to Japan!

Japan is a country rich in history and tradition. Its culture dates back thousands of years. Today, the Japanese islands hold a **unique** blend of Eastern and Western cultures. The country is a leader in technology. Join us and explore the land, history and people of Japan!

Soft drink vending machines are commonplace on the streets in Japanese cities.

The Flag of Japan

The Japanese flag is white with a large red circle in the middle. The circle represents the sun. The Japanese call their country *Nihon*, which means 'source of the sun'. Japan is also known as the 'Land of the Rising Sun'.

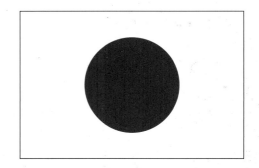

The Land

Japan sits in the Pacific Ocean off the northeastern coast of the Asian continent. The four main islands of Japan—Honshu, Hokkaido, Shikoku, and Kyushu—have breathtaking ocean views and beautiful mountains. The Kanto Plain, on the island of Honshu, is the largest area of flat land in Japan. Many large cities, including Japan's capital, Tokyo, are on the Kanto Plain.

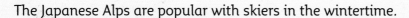

The Japanese Alps are popular with skiers in the wintertime.

The Japanese regard Mount Fuji as a symbol of beauty.

Mount Fuji

Mount Fuji is the tallest mountain in Japan at 3,776 metres. This inactive volcano has not erupted since 1707 and is one of the international symbols of Japan. While some admire Mount Fuji from afar, thousands of people undertake the challenge of climbing it. In winter and spring, the peak is covered with snow.

Climate

The climate of Japan varies widely. In the north, the winters are long and harsh. Sapporo, in the north, has an average winter temperature of –5° Celsius. Further south, the climate is comfortably warm. In Okinawa, the average winter temperature is 15° C.

Maple trees turn bright shades of red, yellow and orange in the autumn.

Cherry trees bloom for less than a week every year in Japan. Many people go to parks to see the blossoms.

The Japanese macaque lives on Honshu, Shikoku and Kyushu. Bushy fur keeps this animal warm in winter.

Plants and Animals

More than 60 per cent of Japan is covered with forest. The trees grow on steep, remote mountains. This makes the trees difficult to chop down and allows them to survive. Japan is one of the most highly forested developed countries.

Japan is home to many unique animals such as the Asiatic brown bear. This bear lives on Honshu, Kyushu and Shikoku. Japan is also home to waterbirds, such as the crane.

History

People from the northern Asian region of Siberia were probably the first group to settle in Japan from about 30,000 BCE. Back then, all four of Japan's main islands were connected, and Hokkaido, in the north, was joined to Siberia. The early people were thus able to migrate easily to Japan simply by crossing the land on foot. By 500 BCE, groups of people from China and Korea–known as the Yayoi–began arriving in Japan.

The Heian Era and Civil War

Kyoto (or Heian-kyo as it was then called) became the capital of Japan in 794. Families, known as clans, fought for land. Leaders of clans were called 'emperors', a title still used today. During the Heian Era (794–1185), the Fujiwara clan controlled the government. In 1192, Minamoto Yoritomo became the military leader of Japan. Fighting continued and a **civil war** began. The Muromachi Period (1333–1573)

Many buildings were ruined during wars for land. The Todaiji Temple in Nara was completely destroyed and then rebuilt in a modern style of architecture.

The *samurai* were military warriors who were skilled in battle and very loyal to their leaders. They fought with weapons like the spear, bow and arrow, gun and, especially, the sword.

was filled with more wars between rival clans which split the central government into independent states.

In the 1500s, Tokugawa Ieyasu united Japan. He expelled foreigners and banned his people from travelling. This **isolation** lasted for more than two hundred years.

These Japanese naval officers are part of the Maritime Self Defense Force. Japan's post-World War II constitution says the country will maintain an exclusive self-defence policy.

Ending Japanese Isolation

Foreigners returned to Japan in 1854 when the American navy arrived, forcing Japan to end its **policy** of isolation. In 1868, Emperor Meiji took power. He **modernized** Japan and introduced railways, state schools and a **constitution** to the country.

Japan at War

Japan's power grew steadily through the 1900s. The country fought and defeated many neighbouring nations including China, Russia and Korea.

Japan entered World War II on 7 December 1941. On that day, it bombed the United States naval base at Pearl Harbor, Hawaii. The war lasted for almost four years. In 1945, the United States destroyed the cities of Hiroshima and Nagasaki with atomic bombs. Japan was devastated and finally surrendered.

Emperor Hirohito was the longest reigning emperor in Japan's history. He ruled the country from 1926 until his death in 1989.

Emperor Meiji's birth name was Prince Musuhito. At fifteen, when he became emperor, he changed his name to Meiji, meaning 'enlightened ruler'.

Murasaki Shikibu (978-1026)

Murasaki Shikibu–or Lady Murasaki–wrote one of the most famous books in Japan, *The Tale of Genji*. It is a story about life in the Heian royal court.

Minamoto Yoritomo (1147-1199)

In 1192, Minamoto Yoritomo became the first **shogun** of Japan. He established a **feudal system** that lasted until the 1800s.

Tokugawa Ieyasu (1543-1616)

This statue of Tokugawa Ieyasu was built in 1617 and can be found at the Toshugu Shrine in the city of Nikko.

In 1600, Tokugawa Ieyasu became the **shogun** of Japan. The Tokugawa clan ruled Japan for over two hundred years.

Emperor Meiji (1852-1912)

In 1868, after a national revolution called the Meiji Restoration, Emperor Meiji became the head of a new **democratic** government. He helped modernize Japan.

The Government and the Economy

Government

After World War II, Japan wrote a new constitution emphasizing the ideas of peace and human rights. The constitution includes a section that says that Japan cannot become a military threat or aggressive power and can only maintain a defensive army.

The prime minister heads Japan's democratic government. He is assisted by members of the Diet, which is the national

The National Diet Building is located in Tokyo.

Elections are held for governors every four years. Candidates travel through cities by bus or tram asking for support from the voters.

Every neighbourhood has a 'police box', which is a miniature police station with one room. People go there for help or to report problems.

legislature, or law-making body, of Japan. The Diet is divided into two chambers— the House of Councillors and the House of Representatives. The Diet makes the national laws.

Japan is divided into forty-seven areas, called **prefectures**. Each prefecture has its own governor and officials. The officials are in charge of maintaining parks and school systems and providing health care.

Japanese workers are loyal to their company and often work at the same job for many years.

Economic Development

Selling products to other countries has made Japan an economic leader in the world. Japan makes many types of goods, such as cars, televisions, computers and cameras for **export**. It continues to spend a lot of money to develop new, high-quality products.

Japanese companies have also built factories in neighbouring South Korea, Hong Kong, Taiwan and Malaysia, where costs are lower.

Energy

Most of Japan's energy comes from hydroelectric and thermal power plants. Hydroelectric power plants make use of moving water to create electricity. Thermal power plants generate electricity by burning fuel such as gas, oil and coal. Japan also depends on nuclear power for about one-third of its electricity. The government expects nuclear power to continue being a major source of energy in the future but it is also developing other alternatives, such as wind and solar power.

Agriculture

Rice is the **staple** food of the Japanese diet. It is expensive to produce and costs more than foreign rice. In 1993, Japan was forced to import rice from other countries when its crops failed.

It is time to **harvest** the rice crop. Farms in Japan are usually small.

People and Lifestyle

Who Lives in Japan?

Japan has the tenth largest population in the world. Around 127 million people live there.

The original people of Japan are the **Ainu** (eye-noo). They are one of several minority groups. The Ainu lived in Japan before people known as the Yayoi began arriving from the Asian continent in 300 BCE.

These girls pose for a picture making a 'V' with their fingers. This is a popular photo pose in Japan.

Tatami (tah-tah-mee) floors are common in Japan. They are made from tightly woven rice stalks and are very soft to walk on.

Types of Building

Large cities such as Tokyo, Osaka and Yokohama are home to over 75 per cent of the population. Most people live in low-rise buildings and work in medium and high-rise buildings.

Japanese Homes

Japanese homes are very small. Most people sleep on futon (foo-ton) bedding on the living room floor. In the morning, the futons are rolled up and stored in a cupboard.

Social relationships and interaction are important to Japanese people.

Belonging to a Group

In Japan, great value is placed on the ability to fit into a group. Groups are important in both work and social situations. They show that people can blend in and get along together.

Growing Up

When a child starts going to school, he or she becomes part of a new group. Children are expected to fit in with others and not break any rules.

Raising a Family

Traditionally, men in Japan work long hours with many late nights. They are expected to earn the money for their family.

When women get married, some of them give up their jobs or work part-time after they have children. This is due to a lack of day-care centres in Japan. There are about 40,000 children on the waiting list. However, there are still more working women in Japan than women who do not work outside the home.

Most Japanese families are small as the birth rate is only one to two children per woman. Unlike other Asian cultures, the Japanese treat both boys and girls equally.

Education

The competition in Japanese schools is strong. Students have to pass difficult tests in order to advance to the next grade. The most difficult exam is the university entrance exam. Some students take the exams many times before passing.

Despite their strong sense of tradition, many modern Japanese women are expected to graduate from universities. Students from top universities often work for the government or the best companies.

Students must deal with the pressures of school from a young age. Doing well in exams is very important.

School Life

Students go to school 240 days a year, with a six-week break in the summer. They have classes from Monday to Friday and a half day on Saturday. Children are also responsible for cleaning their schools.

Cram Schools

Cram schools help students prepare for university entrance exams. Some children attend these schools to make sure they pass their exams.

Shinto and Buddhism

The main religions in Japan are Shinto and Buddhism. *Shinto* (shin-to) means 'ways of the gods'. This religion began in Japan in **prehistoric** times. People often pray at small Shinto shrines at home or go to the numerous shrines found across the country. Buddhism was introduced to Japan in 522 CE. Buddhists believe that when they die, their souls live on and

A Shinto table like this can be found in many Japanese homes. The cat with its raised paw is supposed to bring good luck.

Each year, thousands of people visit this Great Buddha in Kamakura. Buddhists have a positive outlook on death. They believe that when a person dies, his or her soul is born again into a new being.

come back to life again and again. This is called reincarnation. Most Japanese are Buddhist.

Christianity

Only about 2 per cent of Japanese follow the Christian fait'

Language

The spoken Japanese language is made up of simple sounds and grammar. Spoken Japanese is very difficult to learn and may take many years to master.

You must have a great memory to learn Japanese. You need to know over three thousand written characters called *kanji* (kahn-jee) just to read a newspaper!

Books are very popular in Japan. During the twentieth century, Japanese writers Kawabata Yasunari and Oe Kenzaburo both won the Nobel Prize for Literature.

Written Japanese

There are three systems of writing in Japanese–*kanji*, **hiragana** (hee-rah-gah-nah) and **katakana** (kah-tah-kah-nah). *Kanji* was adopted from Chinese culture and it is the most difficult to learn.

Literature

Women wrote the first novels in Japan during the Heian Era (794–1185). *The Tale of Genji* is the most famous of these.

Arts

Crafts

In Japan, highly skilled craftspeople are called 'living national treasures'. The government pays these artists to teach their crafts to other people.

Painting

Older Japanese paintings focus on the events of everyday life and the passing of the seasons. Some families hang these long, painted scrolls in their homes. Today, modern art is also popular in Japan.

These Japanese crafts are bright and colourful. They are also fun to play with!

This historic Japanese painting shows Westerners in Japan. Western European culture was introduced to Japan in the 1540s with the arrival of traders and missionaries from Spain and Portugal.

Calligraphy

Writing Japanese characters with a brush and ink is called calligraphy. This specialized art is taught to schoolchildren.

Prints

Woodblock printing is one of Japan's most famous arts. Carving, painting and pressing the blocks onto paper results in beautiful prints.

Traditional Theatre

In Japanese theatre, the same stories are told again and again so the audience often knows what to expect.

Noh, Bunraku and Kabuki

Noh (no) is an ancient form of Japanese theatre based on religious stories. Actors chant their lines and move their bodies in slow motion. *Bunraku* (boon-rah-koo) mixes storytelling, puppetry and music. The puppets' mouths, eyes and eyebrows all move! *Kabuki* (kah-boo-kee) theatre presents classical Japanese stories of drama with traditional singing and dancing.

Masks used in Japanese theatre.

The puppets in *bunraku* are about 1.2 metres tall.

Popular Japanese singers have huge fan followings, just as singers have in the West.

Film, Television and Music

These popular arts originated in Western culture and have been adapted to suit Japanese tastes. Kurosawa Akira (*The Seven Samurai*) and Itami Juzo (*Tampopo*) are Japan's best-known filmmakers.

Manga and Anime

The Japanese have a distinctive drawing style for still and moving cartoons. Japanese comic books are called *manga* while anime refers to animated shows. Astro Boy is a popular character that has appeared in both manga and anime.

Leisure Time

Time to Relax

A popular hobby with the Japanese is *ikebana* (ee-keh-bah-nah), the art of flower arranging. These flower arrangements are displays of natural beauty.

The tea ceremony is an ancient **ritual** in Japan. The host serves green tea to guests and allows them to enjoy the simple pleasures of nature.

This woman is practising *ikebana*. Each flower is placed very carefully.

Pachinko (pah-cheen-ko) mixes the fun of pinball and slot machines. It is named after the sound the steel balls make in the machine–*pachin!*

Karaoke is a favourite pastime in Japan. At special clubs, people sing along to recorded music. They read the song lyrics off television screens.

The Japanese also enjoy travelling within Japan and to other countries.

Sports

Baseball or **besuboru** (beh-soo-baw-roo) is the most popular team sport in Japan. Japan has two leagues, each with six teams. The Tokyo Giants is the name of the most popular team.

Japanese people of all ages love baseball. Fifteen million citizens attend baseball games every year.

In the Japanese sport of **kendo** (ken-doh), athletes fence with bamboo swords.

Traditional Japanese fighting and self-defense have made way for modern martial arts, such as **karate** and **judo**. Many martial arts competitions take place in Japan.

In 1993, the J-League, Japan's first professional football league, was created. Spectator interest in football has risen greatly ever since Japan qualified for its first World Cup in 1998 and co-hosted the tournament with South Korea in 2002. The national team remains among the best in Asia. During matches enthusiastic fans may pound the traditional *taiko* (tie-co), or Japanese drum to show their support, excitement and pride.

Gion Matsuri

The Gion Matsuri (gee-on-mah-tsoo-ree) festival takes place every year on 17 July. Originally, it was to ask the gods for protection from the plague, a killer disease. Today, the festival has become a traditional celebration.

New Year's Day

The New Year, called Shogatsu (show-gah-tsoo), is the biggest festival of the year in Japan and lasts for three days.

The Gion Matsuri festival began in 876 CE. These musicians ride through town on one of the many floats during the annual parade.

Children's Day is celebrated on 5 May. Banners, such as these, are hung outside Japanese homes and along riverbanks. The carp is a symbol of bravery and strength.

Bon Festival

During the Bon festival, people believe ghosts return to Earth. Floating candles and lanterns are placed on rivers to guide the ghosts back to heaven or hell. Many people return to their hometowns to clean their family graves during Bon.

Food

Japanese Meals

Most Japanese meals are very healthy. Rice is the basis of the Japanese diet–most people eat it at least twice a day. It is so important, in fact, that meals are called 'morning rice', 'noon rice' and 'evening rice'.

Little squares of vinegared rice and raw fish or egg wrapped in seaweed are called **sushi**. Sushi is a popular lunch dish and comes in many varieties.

Few spices are used in Japanese cooking. The food is always fresh and presented in small dishes.

Pizza and pasta are popular alternatives to rice.

Foreign Influences

Through the years, Japan has adopted dishes from other countries—even hamburgers! The foods are changed, however, to fit Japanese tastes. The Japanese top their pizza with squid and seaweed and use Japanese sauces in other foreign dishes.

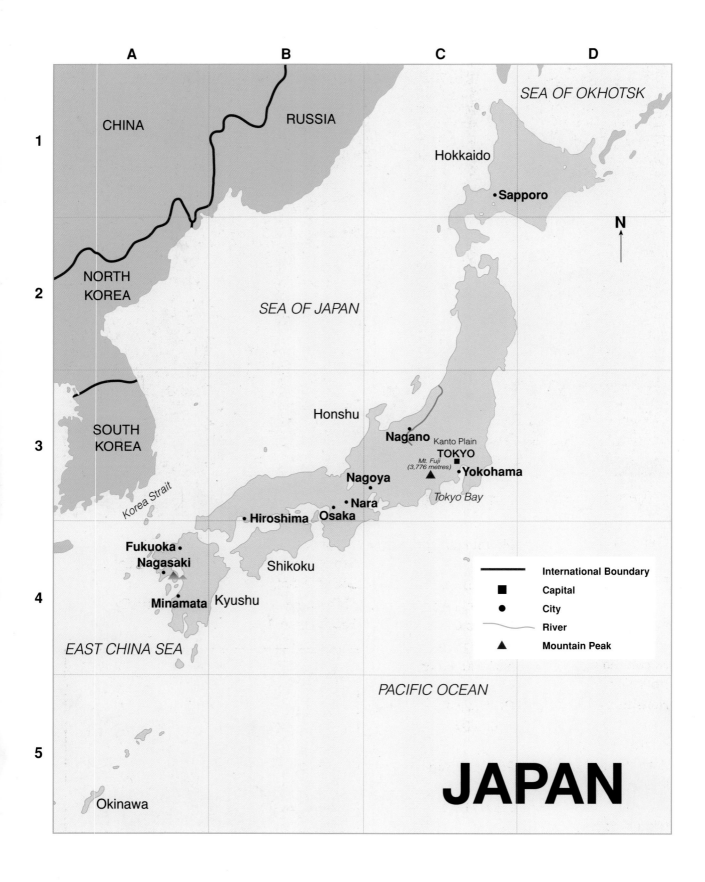

The majestic splendour of Mount Fuji.

China A1

East China Sea A4

Fukuoka A4

Hiroshima B3
Hokkaido C1
Honshu B3

Kanto Plain C3
Korea Strait A3
Kyushu B4

Minamata A4

Mount Fuji C3

Nagano C3
Nagasaki A4
Nagoya C3
Nara B3
North Korea A2

Okinawa A5
Osaka B3

Pacific Ocean C5

Russia B1

Sapporo C1
Sea of Japan B2
Sea of Okhotsk D1
Shikoku B4
South Korea A3

Tokyo C3
Tokyo Bay C3

Yokohama C3

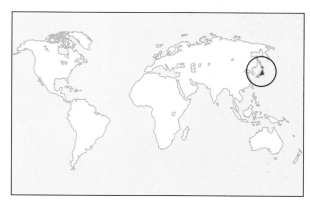

Quick Facts

Official Name Japan (Nihon)

Capital Tokyo

Official Language Japanese

Population 127 million

Land Area 364,485 square kilometres

Largest Islands Hokkaido, Honshu, Kyushu, Shikoku

Highest Point Mount Fuji (3,776 metres)

Main Religions Buddhism, Shinto

Major Festivals New Year's Day, Children's Day, Bon, Gion Matsuri

Major Cities Tokyo, Osaka, Yokohama

Ethnic Groups Japanese and Ainu (98.5 per cent), Korean (0.5 per cent), Others (1 per cent)

National Flower Cherry blossom

National Flag White with a large red circle (representing the sun) in the centre

Currency Japanese Yen (¥136.08 = £1 in 2010)

Japan has one of the fastest aging populations in the world but a low birthrate so couples are being encouraged to have more children.

Glossary

Ainu: the original people of Japan

besuboru: baseball

bunraku: traditional puppet theatre

civil war: a conflict between people from the same country

constitution: the laws or principles of a nation

democratic: describing a country with a government elected by its people

export: a product that is made for the purpose of selling to another country

feudal system: a type of political organization in which a subject gave service to a lord and received protection and land in return

harvest: to gather crops

hiragana: Japanese alphabet, used for Japanese words and grammar

ikebana: the art of flower arranging

isolation: the state of being alone

judo: a form of martial arts

kabuki: a form of classical theatre

kanji: Japanese written characters that originated in China

karaoke: singing to recorded music

karate: a martial art

katakana: Japanese phonetic alphabet

kendo: Japanese fencing with bamboo swords

legislature: a body of politicians responsible for making the law

modernize: to update or make new

noh: a form of classical theatre

pachinko: a type of pinball game

policy: a strategy or rule made by the government

prefectures: governed districts

prehistoric: before recorded history

ritual: a ceremony or practice

samurai: a Japanese warrior

shogun: a Japanese military leader

staple: a main or important part of something

sushi : raw fish or seafood on a bite-sized mound of vinegared rice

tatami: a traditional type of flooring in Japan that is made of soft rice straw

unique: special, found in no other place

For More Information

Books

Brooks, Susie. *Japan: In the Children's Own Words*. Our Lives, Our World series. London: Chrysalis Children's Books, 2004

Goulding, Sylvia. *Japan*. Food and Celebrations series. London: Wayland, 2008

Parker, Vicky. *We're from Japan*. London: Heinemann Library, 2006

Reynolds, Betty. *Japanese Celebrations. Cherry Blossoms, Lanterns and Stars!* Tokyo: Tuttle Publishing, 2006

Sato, Shozo. *Tea Ceremony*. Asian Arts and Crafts for Creative Kids series. Tokyo: Tuttle Publishing, 2005

Storey, Rita. *Judo*. Know Your Sport series. London: Franklin Watts, 2007

Tidmarsh, Celia. *Japan*. World in Focus series. London: Wayland, 2008

DVDs

Discovery Atlas: Japan Revealed. (Discovery Channel, 2008).

Rudy Maxa's World: Japan. (Questar, 2009).

Samurai Japan: A Journey Back in Time. (Kultur Video, 2006).

The Little Travelers Japan. (Little Travelers Productions, 2008).

Websites

www.activityvillage.co.uk/japan_for_kids_culture.htm

Learn more about unique Japanese dolls and figurines, Children's Day in Japan and the sports of sumo wrestling as well as martial arts.

factsanddetails.com/japan.php?itemid=1065

Get an insight into Japan's unique pop culture and its many fads and trends from the 1960s to the present day.

www.travelforkids.com/Funtodo/Japan/japan.htm

Find out about the various attractions in selected Japanese cities such as Tokyo, Kyoto and Chugoko. Also has a recommended reading list for children.

web-japan.org/kidsweb

Read essential facts about Japan, with write-ups about its lifestyle, culture and traditions.

Note to parents and teachers: Every effort has been made by the Publishers to ensure that these websites are suitable for children, that they are of the highest educational value, and that they contain no inappropriate or offensive material. However, because of the nature of the Internet, it is impossible to guarantee that the contents of these sites will not be altered. We strongly advise that Internet access is supervised by a responsible adult.

Index